First published 2010 by
Veritas Publications
7–8 Lower Abbey Street
Dublin 1
Ireland
publications@veritas.ie
www.veritas.ie

ISBN 978 1 84730 223 6

10 9 8 7 6 5 4 3 2 1

Designed by Kelly Sheridan, Outsource Graphix Ltd, Dublin
Printed in the Republic of Ireland by Walsh Colour Print, Kerry

Veritas books are printed on paper made from the wood pulp of managed forests. For every tree felled, at least one tree is planted, thereby renewing natural resources.

About the Authors

Fiona McAuslan holds a Masters in Mediation and Conflict Resolution Studies from University College Dublin. She is an experienced mediator and conflict coach with many years' experience working with family, workplace and school conflicts. She works in the Irish Family Mediation Service and Clanwilliam Institute and is an accredited Practitioner Mediator with the Mediators Institute of Ireland. Fiona has published the S.A.L.T. Programme: A Conflict Resolution Education Programme for Primary schools. She lives in North County Dublin with her husband, Michael, and two children, Sarah and Ben.

Peter Nicholson is a communications specialist and has built a very successful Marketing and Visual Communications Business over the last fifteen years. Peter and Fiona met whilst working on the S.A.L.T. programme and they have continued to work together on many other projects. He is married to Karen, and they have two children, Patrick and Ailish.

About the Illustrator

Kelly Sheridan studied Classical and Computer Animation in Ballyfermot College of Further Education for three years before attending the Irish Academy of Computer Training (IACT) to study Graphic Design and Desktop Publishing. A keen illustrator and life drawer, she loves the work of Tim Burton and Walter Sickert. Originally from Crumlin, Kelly currently lives in Tallaght with her partner, Mark.

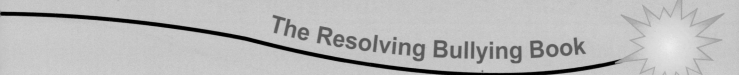

Read Me First!

This is not just another story book, it's a Tool Book. So what's a Tool Book then? It's a book that explains an issue, shows how children can be affected by it and how they can resolve the problem. It also offers a number of tips and techniques that can be used again and again to improve the ability to deal with Bullying on a day-to-day basis.

Section 1
What is Bullying?
This is a simple explanation of what Bullying is.

Section 2
The Story
The story helps the reader identify Bullying in their world and helps open the door to discussing and resolving the issue.

Section 3
Tool Box
The Tool Box has many tips and techniques that can be used in everyday life on an ongoing basis. The more they are practised, the better the result!

What is Bullying?

- Bullying is more than bad behaviour. It is when somebody does things to make someone else feel bad about themselves.

- It might be calling somebody names, hitting or kicking them, or just doing mean things.

- Whatever the bully does, it makes the other person feel miserable.

- The bully seems big and powerful to the other person. They seem to control what the person thinks and does.

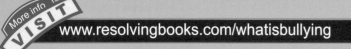
More info VISIT www.resolvingbooks.com/whatisbullying

What is Bullying?

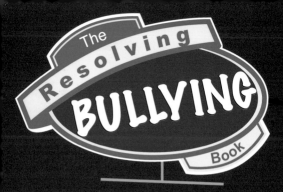
The Resolving BULLYING Book

How Bullying Can Make You Feel

Moody

Anxious

Nervous

Stressed

Ill

Lonely

Clingy

Unconfident

Aggressive

Signs of Being Bullied

Having Nightmares

Can't Sleep

Being Tired

Over-eating

Being Withdrawn

Not Hungry

Bed-wetting

Not able to Concentrate

What is Bullying?

7

The Resolving BULLYING Book

What Happens Inside

When we get anxious our brain floods with chemicals, which switch off the language centre in our brain.

- We cannot think clearly.
- We feel nervous.
- We find it hard to know what to do.

More info VISIT www.resolvingbooks.com/whathappensinside

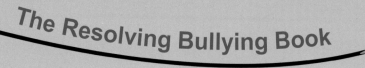

When we are being bullied, every time we think about or see the other person our brain floods with adrenalin. It can become a habit. We feel anxious and we can't think clearly.

What is Bullying?

This is Dan

Dan has lots of friends.
He likes to play games with them.

He listens to people and
tells good jokes.

3rd

Dan began not to like school.

He woke up one morning with a horrible feeling in his tummy.

I'm being silly. School is fun. I'll be ok.

But as he walked to school, he felt sicker and sicker. He didn't talk to his friends anymore. He walked a bit behind them. What was wrong with Dan?

Dan stopped playing games because he thought he wasn't very good at them. He stopped telling jokes. He wasn't very happy.

He stayed on his own.

He didn't play with anyone.

He thought he was no good as a friend.

Dan hated how he felt. He hated his hair. He hated his life.

Bullying is when somebody does things to make someone else feel bad about themselves.

It might be calling somebody names, hitting or kicking them or just doing mean things.

Whatever they do, it makes the other person feel miserable.

He wants you to be scared of him.

He wants you to feel bad and he wants you to have no friends.

Tell her what you have told me. It gets easier each time you talk about it.

Tell her:
1. What has happened.
2. Who is doing it.
3. How often it has happened.
4. If anyone else saw or heard what went on.
5. What you have tried to do about it so far.

Ok, I'll do it. I'll let you know how I get on.

That's good, but you can't keep losing your lunch.
I know. My Mum is going to talk to my teacher. Mum's told me that Bobby will not even know that she's been to the school.
That's great, and there is still more you can do to help yourself.

Mediator

Listens

The Caterpillar

- The Caterpillar in the story plays the part of a mediator. The questions he asks and the way he listens are all done using mediation skills.

- A mediator does not judge people or take sides. Their role is to use their skills to help people resolve their own conflict. They do this by listening to each person, asking questions and using negotiation techniques to help the person think and learn about what they are feeling.

- The mediator helps them to talk to each other and to understand each other's point of view. In doing so, they can find a way forward together.

Stays Cool

Helps Find Solutions

Remains Impartial

Understands

Doesn't Judge

Asks Good Questions

Tool Box

59

The Caterpillar Helped Because...

Listening helps calm kids.

Listening helps kids work things out for themselves.

Good questions help kids talk about what really bothers them.

Focusing on them helps kids think about their own thoughts and feelings.

Helping kids sort it out for themselves helps them learn to be better friends.

Skills used by the Caterpillar in this story:

1. **Listening** to what Dan felt and why he was upset is a more effective way of helping him learn from his situation. If he was simply told what to do, he would not have had the opportunity to learn about what had happened to him and how to handle this better in the future. When Dan felt listened to, he was more able to do something about it. He opened up and talked about what was really bothering him.

2. The **questions** the Caterpillar asks helps Dan talk about what really bothers him and makes a big difference in how he understands the real nature of bullying.

3. The Caterpillar does not talk about himself. He **concentrates on Dan**. This means he has to focus on his own thoughts and feelings.

4. **The Caterpillar does not sort out the problem**. He leaves that to Dan, who at the end of the day learns more from thinking it through himself. The Caterpillar empowers Dan by supporting him in this way.

All the skills and ideas that the Caterpillar uses can be used by anyone reading this story.

A Bully

A Bully is tough.
A Bully is strong.
A Bully is brave.
A Bully is fearless.
A Bully is better.
A Bully is tall.

The truth is... they are not at all!

A Bully is weak.
A Bully is cowardly.
A Bully is worse.
A Bully is small... that's all!

Sarah Jones (13)

Bullies

People who bully do it to feel better about themselves. They feel good when they have power over somebody else.

Feeling **bigger** than someone else makes them forget how small they feel inside.

Bullies want others to pay them lots of attention and to think about how cool, smart, big or strong they are.

Listening and Talking

The most important thing to do when somebody has been bullied is to listen to them.

As listeners, we need to help the other person express themselves better so that we can truly understand them.

What's wrong?	I don't know
You seem sad	Yes, I'm unhappy
Tell me more	I had a bad day
What happened?	Well, Bobby stole my lunch

What did you think when he did that?

 I wanted him to leave me alone

 How did you feel?

 I was really scared

 What was the hardest thing?

 I had to tell my teacher and I'm worried Bobby will do it again

 What do you think needs to happen now?

 I don't know. I want Bobby to stop. Maybe I could tell my friends

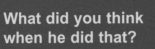

Remember:
It is important to talk about how you feel. Listening and talking helps us calm our minds and think more clearly.

It can help us decide what to do.

What To Do

Do talk to parents, someone in your family, a teacher, a helpline.

Don't hit back with violence.   **Don't** get into a fight.

1. Tell someone you trust, maybe a friend.

2. Ask them to help you.

3. Ask them to come with you to tell an adult.

4. Ask them to stand alongside you.

More info VISIT www.resolvingbooks.com/helpline

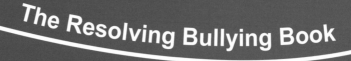

When You Talk To Someone

Tell them:

1. What has happened.

2. Who is doing it.

3. How often it has happened.

4. If anyone else saw or heard what went on.

5. What you have tried to do about it so far.

Remember:

People who bully want you to feel bad about yourself. Don't give them that power.

The best defence is to:

• Like yourself.
• Be confident in yourself.
• Don't believe the bully.
• Don't hit back with violence. You can't force someone who
  is a bully into not being a bully.

**Bullying is about others who want to have power
and control over you.**

What Can Parents / Adults Do?

As the saying goes, prevention is better than cure. Discuss bullying behaviour with children so that they become aware of what kind of effects it can have. Failure to act gives a silent but strong message that aggressive behaviour is ok and acceptable.

Be aware of your own behaviour and lead by example.

Encourage children to report incidents. Make sure they know that it is always right to tell when they see something wrong.

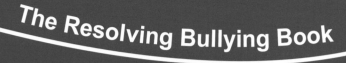

If you think a child is being bullied, encourage them to:

• Act as confident as they can.

• Face the bully and tell them clearly to stop.

• Try to be calm and move away from the bully.

Also remind the child of the following:

• Don't hit back. You may get hurt or the bully can use it against you.

• Bullies like to get a reaction; if they don't get one, there is no point in them bullying you.

• If they call you names, try to laugh it off. Don't let them see that they have hurt you.

• Never try to beat a bully at their own game.

• If you need help, tell an adult you know and trust.

Strong Words

When we are being bullied we stop knowing what to say. Here are some useful things to say:

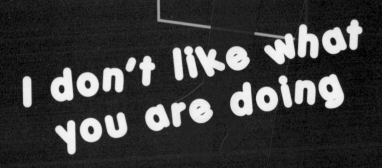

I don't like what you are doing

Go away

No. Leave me alone!

Stop!

Write your own things to say on the wall:

Learning to be Strong

It can take time to learn new things. We need to practise and slowly we will get better at it.

Remember:

1. It is not your fault.

2. Look for help.

3. Stand tall.

4. Look the bully in the eye.

5. Try not to show that you are upset.

Practise:

1. Taking big breaths to stay calm.

2. Using strong words.

3. Looking brave, even when you are scared.

4. Thinking of what makes you special.

Rehearsal Room

Tool Box

73

What Should I Do If I See Someone Else Being Bullied?

1. Tell an adult. They will help you sort out what is happening.

2. Remember that talking to an adult about bullying is not telling tales.

3. Ask the person being bullied to play with you and your friends.

4. Play fair - don't let the bully change the way you behave.

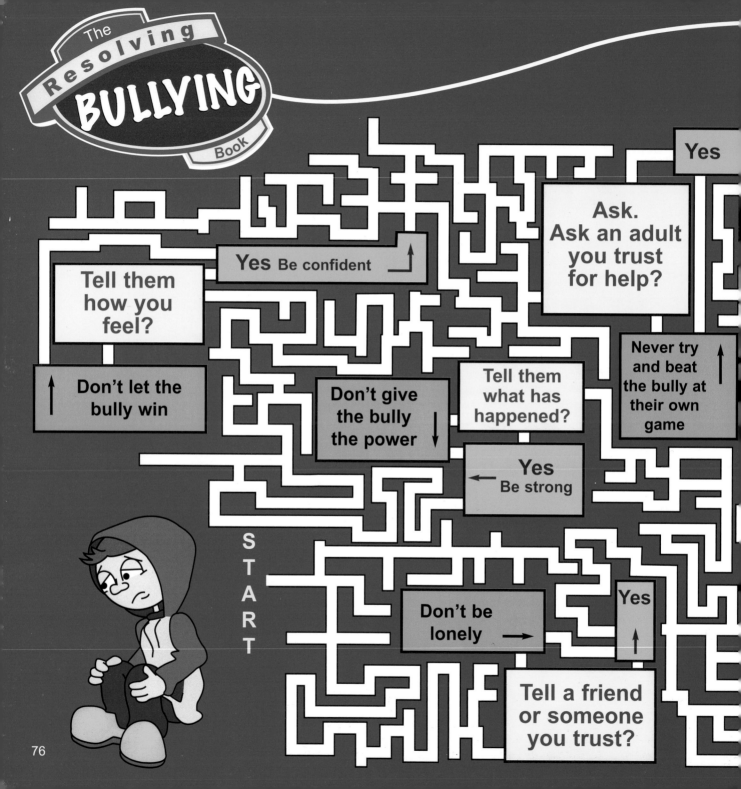